Joining *the* Conversation

Joining *the* Conversation

2019
Seabeck Haiku Getaway
Anthology

C. R. Manley, editor

Haiku Northwest Press

Haiku Northwest Press
Bellevue, Washington

Copyright © 2020 by Haiku Northwest
Cover image and haiga © 2020 by Ion Codrescu

All rights revert to the authors and artist upon publication of this book. No part of this book may be used or reproduced in any manner whatsoever without written permission from the contributor, except in the case of brief quotations in reviews.

This collection of poems commemorates Haiku Northwest's 12th annual Seabeck Haiku Getaway, held October 24–27, 2019 at the Seabeck Conference Center in Seabeck, Washington.

Layout and design by C. R. Manley
with assistance from Michael Dylan Welch

ISBN 978-1-953092-02-1

Poems and prose set in Constantia.
Titles and headings set in Myriad Pro.

www.haikunorthwest.org

Paying Attention	7
Rengay	17
Haiku and Senryu	21
Kukai Winners	69
Seabeck Haiku Walk	77
Poets and Places	93

Paying Attention

The 12th annual Seabeck Haiku Getaway took place October 24–27, 2019 at the Seabeck Conference Center in Seabeck, Washington, on the shores of Hood Canal.

We shared the Seabeck campus with other groups: high school students attending a jazz workshop, and at least one group of quilters, busy at their sewing machines in another building. As is usual for Seabeck in late autumn, we were gifted with some rain, some wind, and some colorful leaves.

Michael Dylan Welch did a wonderful job planning the getaway so that nearly every minute offered something interesting, inspiring, or provocative. Angela Terry's organizational skills ensured that everything ran smoothly—or as smoothly as possible for an event with more than 65 haiku poets in attendance.

The theme of the 2019 getaway was "paying attention"—to what you experience in your life, the haiku you write, and the haiku you read. Many presentations and activities connected with and expanded on this theme during the weekend.

The getaway featured two guests of honor:

- Adam L. Kern, a professor of Japanese Literature and Visual Culture at the University of Wisconsin-Madison, the editor and translator of *The Penguin Book of Haiku*, and the author of books about Edo-era manga and 17th- and 18th-century Japanese literature.

- Ion Codrescu, of Constanța, Romania, the author of 16 books of poetry, haiga, and essays, and an artist who has illustrated more than 125 books, magazines, and newspapers, and has had work in more than 50 exhibitions around the world.

Thursday

Attendees began arriving on the afternoon of Thursday, October 24. We reunited with old friends and met new ones during check-in at the Historic Inn, and under Barbara Snow's direction created haiku weathergrams to hang around the Seabeck grounds.

After dinner the formal program began with a round of introductory haiku readings, which Gary Evans videorecorded (available on Haiku Northwest's YouTube channel). We also enjoyed an energetic "common ground" icebreaker led by Michael, which was a sort of musical-chairs exercise where we had to repeatedly swap seats with others with whom we shared something in common, such as being from out of state or having visited Japan.

Adam L. Kern then introduced his book with a reading of poems titled, "A Brisk Waddle through *The Penguin Book of Haiku*." In the first of many "Write Now" prompts during the getaway, Michael asked each person to draw a slip of paper from a basket—but in fact each prompt was the same: "penguin." And so we created a virtual "book" of penguin haiku.

In this anthology you'll find a poem written from Michael's penguin prompt, and you'll also find poems written from the verbal prompts of the presenters of the other "Write Now" exercises throughout the weekend who helped us stretch our writing muscles and reminded us that inspiration can come from almost anywhere:

- Jacob Salzer: "The Digital Sea"—the technology in our lives
- Jim Rodriguez: "The Last Meal You Ate"
- Lynne Jambor: "Toy Stories"
- Jacquie Pearce: "All the News That Fits"
- Kelly Sauvage Angel: "Secret Loves and Guilty Pleasures"
- Terry Ann Carter: "Paying Attention to Light: A Homage to Lawrence Ferlinghetti" (with piano improvisation)
- Margaret Chula: "The Fedora in the Room"—what we were wearing, and clothes in general
- Carmen Sterba: "The Heart of a Child"—memories from our childhoods
- Roy Kindelberger: "Haiku On My Mind"—a photograph or song that's stuck in your head

Michael then talked about "Haiku Battle: Comparing Western Haiku Animation and Japanese Haiku Anime" and showed video clips of "Sokka's Haiku Battle" from *Avatar—The Last Airbender* (an American animated series) and a haiku episode from the *Crossing Time* anime series (from Japan). The resulting discussion highlighted differences between American and Japanese perspectives on both animation and haiku, and this served as a prelude to other presentations during the getaway.

The evening finished up with time for a late-night anonymous workshop.

Friday

After breakfast, the presentations continued with two talks that explored Western comics, manga, and haiku. "Comic Relief: The Intersection of Comics and Haiku" was led by Michael with commentary by Adam. Using pages of newspaper comics, participants identified similarities between comics and haiku, such as having three panels and the use of implication. That was followed by "Co-mixing Cultures East and West: The Shocking Transnational Affair of Japanese Manga and Euroamerican Comics," in which Adam described how the invention of modern Japanese manga resulted from the intermingling of Japanese woodblock printed comics and Western editorial cartoons.

Port Townsend poet, essayist, and art critic Christine Hemp then presented "From Homer to #hashtags: Our

Changing Language." She discussed how the digital age is transforming how we write and converse—and how changes in language affect the way we think and feel about our world, our history, ourselves, and haiku. Christine's presentation was sponsored by the Humanities Washington Speakers Bureau.

Five authors then read their poems, some of which came from recently published books: Marco Fraticelli, "Saying Goodbye"; Pat Benedict, *The Alchemy of Tea*; William Scott Galasso, *Rough Cut: Thirty Years of Senryu*; Jacquie Pearce and Angela Terry, *A New Resonance 11*; and Ion Codrescu, "By the Mountain Trail."

In a workshop titled "Snap to Haiku," kjmunro guided us as we used postcards as visual prompts in combination with our immediate surroundings, our memories, and our senses. Following that, craft supplies were provided for us to create collage haiga using our own poems, then Terry Ann Carter and Marco Fraticelli led an anonymous critique session.

Sociality in the writing of haiku was the focus of the next two presentations. In "Sado Island: My Renku Journey in Japan," Ion Codrescu explored the theory and sociality of collaborative writing as reflected in a half-kasen renku he had written with others more than twenty years ago on a visit to Japan. Richard Tice then talked about how "English-Language Haiku Poets Are Missing Out on All the Fun: Sociality in Haiku"—haiku and haikai were a product of interactive composition and social interaction in Japan for hundreds of years until the late 1800s.

Connie Hutchison's "Remembering Mary Fran Meer" honored a long-time member of Haiku Northwest who passed in July of 2019, and Barbara memorialized Mary Fran's haiku on weathergrams, which we tied to a bush outside our meeting room.

After dinner, two presentations touched on Chinese art and literature and their connections to Japan. Sheila Sondik's "My Chinese Literati Art Journey" was an illustrated exploration of Chinese and Japanese art forms and how they influenced her own visual art. David Berger's "The Library Cave and the Silk Road's Dunhuang Cave Temples" described the early 1900s' archeological find of more than 40,000 works on paper and silk that changed understandings of the Silk Road and of Buddhist culture and literature.

Friday night ended with time for rengay.

Saturday

The weekend brings additional attendees who could not be present during the workweek. With this in mind, the Saturday schedule has traditionally included special activities and events. After breakfast, Angela welcomed everyone and kicked off the day with a round of introductions that included the new arrivals.

In the morning's first presentation, "Matsuo Bashō and Pieter Brueghel: Two Approaches to Nature," Ion Codrescu examined how the poems of Bashō and the artwork of Brueghel reflect what they learned from nature—

and described how we could use that approach to deepen our attention to haiku.

Michael introduced Girl's Day and Boy's Day traditions with a brief talk about his display of "Emperor Dolls and Samurai Helmets." Richard Tice then explained that in Japan, Children's Day has long been observed as the two holidays, March 3 for girls and May 5 for boys, and has inspired haiku for centuries. He then read and discussed a selection of "Girl's Day and Boy's Day Haiku."

In "Giving Attention to Haiku in Mary Oliver's Poetry," Michael explored what her poetry can teach haiku poets about paying close attention to our experiences and emotions—as exemplified by a stanza from her poem "Sometimes": "Instructions for living a life: Pay attention. Be astonished. Tell about it."

After lunch, Adam's talk "Haiku vs. Senryu: How to Tell the Difference—And Why It Doesn't Matter!" upended the perennial debate of where to draw the line between these two forms by revealing a larger, historical perspective.

Tanya McDonald introduced the 2019 Porad Haiku Award and profiled its namesake, Francine Porad, who founded Haiku Northwest (which sponsors the award). The winning poems, judged by Tom Painting, were read aloud by contest coordinator Ron Swanson, with flute music by Jim Rodriguez. Unlike in many previous years, none of the winners were present at the getaway.

After a group photo on the steps of the Meeting House, Angela and Michael led us on the official launch of the "Seabeck Haiku Walk," a permanent installation around the Seabeck Conference Center grounds of twenty plaques with haiku by Haiku Northwest members (the Haiku Walk poems are included near the end of this anthology). This installation was the culmination of several years of work, and Haiku Northwest is deeply grateful to the Seabeck Conference Center for providing a permanent home for these haiku. To guide generations of future visitors, a "Haiku Walk" handout, produced by the Seabeck Conference Center, will be available in the Historic Inn.

The brisk wind that challenged our hearing (and hair) during the launch of the Haiku Walk led to the subsequent readings, some from recent books, being moved from the Campfire Circle to the Meeting House. Readers were Crystal Simone Smith, "Shorelines: Escape vs. Escape"; Margaret Chula, *One Leaf Detaches*; kjmunro, *Contractions*; Lynne Jambor, "A Year in Poetry"; Marco Fraticelli, *A Thousand Years: The Haiku and Love Letters of Chiyo-ni* (accompanied on flute by Terry Ann Carter). Gary Evans's video of these readings is available on Haiku Northwest's YouTube channel.

Michael then led a lively panel with Margaret Chula, Tanya McDonald, Crystal Simone Smith, and John Stevenson, about "Paying Attention." Panelists shared a poem of their own and explored how attention played a role in its writing. They also discussed how attention is necessary not just in the writer but also in the reader.

The 6:00 pm dinner bell marked the deadline to enter up to two anonymous haiku or senryu per person for our annual anonymous kukai (haiku contest). After dinner the entries were laid out for voting, the results tallied, and the highest-ranked poems read aloud (those kukai poems with nine votes or more are included near the end of this anthology). Winners selected journal and art book prizes generously donated by Jim Rodriguez.

Another long-standing getaway tradition is the Seabeck Talent Show, led this year by intrepid MCs Alphonse and Gaston (aka Pat Benedict and Vicki McCullough). Music, dance, costumes, and silliness! We also enjoyed our annual "sing-off" of poems by our featured guests, with many participants drawing poems from a hat and spontaneously singing them in styles as various as country, opera, and heavy metal.

The evening ended with a late-night rengay session that veered into the erotic—and thus remained anonymous.

Sunday

After breakfast, Adam presented "Dirty Sexy Haiku," an eye-opening examination of a major—if little acknowledged—mode of haiku, in its anatomically correct splendor. Adam shared the anonymous rengay from the night before, and they fit right in with his presentation.

Crystal then led a workshop on "Paying Attention to Achieve Successful Haiku." She explained that if we pay attention to our experiences and also to the approaches we take to record them, successful haiku are not only possible, but inevitable.

With the conclusion of the 2019 Seabeck Haiku Getaway after lunch, we headed out via cars, ferries, and planes for homes in other towns, other states, and other countries—but I hope the haiku, senryu, and rengay collected here remind you of friends you made and experiences you paid attention to during the getaway.

Thank You

We are extremely grateful to Ion Codrescu, who not only graciously created the seven beautiful, varied haiga for selected poems in these pages, but also provided this anthology's colorful cover—a scene instantly familiar to anyone who has spent time in the Seabeck Meeting House.

And many thanks to everyone who attended the getaway and contributed to making this anthology an enjoyable and inspiring souvenir of our time together in Seabeck.

C. R. Manley

Rengay

Vantastic Voyage
Rengay on the Way to Seabeck

morning drizzle—
ready to go by van
to a haiku event
                Ion Codrescu

Vancouver to Mount Baker
two clouds away
                Julie Emerson

inhaling
double-shot vanilla
and pumpkin spice lattes
                Vicki McCullough

rush hour traffic
the HOV lane
an advantage
                kjmunro

the border vanishing
in the distance
                Jacquie Pearce

advancing on Seabeck
fog lifts
from the lagoon
                lynnej

Haiku and Senryu

joining the conversation

sound of rain

Jacob Salzer

Jon Codrescu

joining
the conversation
sound of rain

    Jacob Salzer

white mushrooms
shine in the night drizzle
far-off laughter

    Richard Tice

Seabeck path—
somebody plays a flute
on the porch

> *in memory of Francine Porad*
> Ion Codrescu

below the treeline
just knowing they are there
the brothers

> Bob Redmond

Romanian guests . . .
is a glimpse of our mountains
enough?

> Barbara Snow

mirror pond
the beauty of the forest
doubled

    Patrick Gallagher

toes a-wriggle
we await
the mud sharks

    Kelly Sauvage Angel

wild geese in flight
persistent rain on my windshield
autumn equinox

    Susan M. Callan

icebreaker
on the haiku path
wild berries

    William Scott Galasso

twenty steps
into the forest—
the things I can't name

    C. R. Manley

witch's butter
glows on black logs—
almost Halloween

    Sheila Sondik

hillside hike—
the aspens seem more yellow
in the fog

    Michael Dylan Welch

leaf-covered path—
a single maple seed
nestles in

    Gary Evans

how afternoon light
turns to dusk
berry trail

    Terry Ann Carter

gale-force winds
the mud sharks settle
on the bottom

    lynnej

whitecaps—
one breaks
into an eagle

    Tanya McDonald

pinwheels
on the child's grave
spring wind

    Margaret Chula

no leaves
to see the wind
I watch clouds

    Marco Fraticelli

wind chimes
all the weather forecast
I need

    Laura Quindt

rainfall euphony . . .
the weather vane
at rest

    Vicki McCullough

autumn rain—
the red of forgotten
apples

    Kathleen I. Tice

the house
almost as many angles
as me

    jim rodriguez

three o'clock am—
soft footsteps
on the cold hard floor

    Mike Freiling

time to go in
we follow
the
fireflies
home

Jon Codrescu   Roy Kindelberger

time to go in
we follow the fireflies
home

    Roy Kindelberger

hot summer night
reading in bed
sputtering candle

    Marilyn Stablein

grandpa's pipe smoke
drifts into the milky way
bonfire stories

    Garry Wilson

black and white
the color of
science fiction

    Theresa J. Barker

the faded line
it left behind—
mother's ring

    Bob Redmond

agent orange
the cause my father claims
for all his troubles

    R. J. Swanson

remembering
the taste of lemon pie
IV line drip drip drip

    Laura Quindt

just
enough
pink   for remembrance

    Dianne Garcia

wishing well
I ask for a penny
as the women talk of roses

Carmen Sterba

old school—
he dips my pigtail
into the inkwell

Ida Freilinger

spitting
watermelon seeds at my shadow
summer afternoon

David Berger

blowing the kelp horn
summoning my father
and his knife

Jim Roberts

school out—
I ask my grandpa
to take me to the library

Carmen Sterba

returning in fall . . .
where my grandparents lived
no one's home

Carmi Soifer

the old warmth
as I zip up
my long-lost sweater

    Rick Clark

his easy living mismatched socks

    Sheila Sondik

my flannel shirt
among the white coats
rare bird sighting

    Paul Sarvasy

mountain magic
Alps embellish
Brueghel's Dutch landscapes

Diane Wallihan

the bats out
before the stars—small fish plash
the darkening river

Rick Clark

penguin
underwater
no longer a waddler

Joan Prefontaine

where did the day go?
forty likes on Facebook
two new friends

    Carolyn Winkler

early spring
the chirp-chirping
of my key fob

    Adam L. Kern

disconnected
my phone at the bottom
of my lunch box

    jim rodriguez

when
a word
was technology

    John Stevenson

big dipper
sending the itinerary
to myself

    Crystal Simone Smith

lunch interruption
a delightful call
from his banana phone

    Katharine Grubb

Girls' Day
the youngest daughter
adds her rag doll

Diane Wallihan

Hello Kitty
in seventeen brush strokes
a little girl's world

Angela Terry

summer vacation
cat's eye ricochets
off a steely

R. J. Swanson

Cracker Jacks
the sharp crunch
of a plastic ring

    Margaret Chula

last meal in my teeth

    John Stevenson

laughing loudly
that the loneliness
might be forgotten

    Chigusa
    translated by Adam L. Kern

spring rain
after the lecture on dirty haiku
not just spring rain

Joan Prefontaine

flipping the "r": *bareku,* bodyku, bawdyku

Connie Hutchison

a crisp
clear stillness
yesterday's
tumult

forgiven

Paul Sarvasy

Jon Codrescu

a crisp clear stillness
yesterday's tumult
forgiven

Paul Sarvasy

Johnny Baranski—
his spirit still lingers
in the morning mist

Mike Freiling

lost flashlight
the tire swing now still
yellow dawn

    Katharine Grubb

glee in the morning   yoga

    Theresa J. Barker

breakfast bells
geese fly away
over the moon

    Carole Slesnick

explaining the difference
between sugar and honey
morning moon

    Terry Ann Carter

her precise pour
of milk—
the offer of solace

    Dianne Garcia

oatmeal with brown sugar—
autumn so much
a part of the taste

    Angela Terry

words on plaques
the spirit of friends
   lives on

    William Scott Galasso

hair in the wind
she reads her poem
to shadows

    Garry Wilson

autumn day
nothing good or bad
just a woolly bear

    after Shiki
    Kathleen I. Tice

mid-afternoon
conference coffee break—
just time to pour a cup

    kjmunro

cathedral in the woods—
I find a stump
just my size

    Carole MacRury

writers' retreat
a pen left behind
in the restroom

    Seren Fargo

dinner bell
I opt for a banana
and a nap

    Pat Benedict Campbell

my letter to you
in the playground—
deer

    Julie Emerson

everything darkened
by rain   except
the yellow tire swing

    Vicki McCullough

talent show rehearsal—
the bat flits
to the stage

    kjmunro

late night rengay
the sake sippers call
uncle on the title

    Michelle Schaefer

morning after
reconsidering
the taste of sake

    Jacquie Pearce

cold ginko walk
through watery eyes
the seascape

    Crystal Simone Smith

twofold awareness
warm sun
cold air

    Ellen Ankenbrock

sea lions crossing the sound of crashing waves

    Susan Constable

the space between

the moment

and

the words

Connie Hutchison

Ion Codrescu

the space
between the moment
and the words

    Connie Hutchison

autumn morning
an old oak tree
leans into me

    Jacob Salzer

windy path
a leaf overtakes
a pine cone

> *Seren Fargo*

overcast
geese
sounds

> *Marco Fraticelli*

some deer ignore
for a few moments
the traveler

> *Ion Codrescu*

conscious of us
the octopus stays away—
empty clamshells

    Julie Emerson

cold wind on the lagoon—
the brittle star
hugging itself

    C. R. Manley

mussel shell
washed ashore
barnacle too

    Marilyn Stablein

each year
under the leaves
the dead lie deeper

    Patrick Gallagher

forest walk
after one mushroom
all the others

    Jacquie Pearce

searching for a path
we follow
the dinner gongs

    Carole Slesnick

propped up in bed
to see the incandescent maples
once more

 David Berger

atonal jazz band
the mating call of geese
and fallen apples

 Kelly Sauvage Angel

out-of-tune piano
their fingers caressing music
from each key

 Michelle Schaefer

poetry reading
with no microphone
empty seed pods

    Barbara Snow

ten-minute break
between sessions . . .
bathroom or coffee?

    Pat Benedict Campbell

haiku heaven
haiku hell
the same

    Carolyn Winkler

windfall apples—
the deer and I
freeze

    Carole MacRury

forest bathing
red maples with a hint
of woodsmoke

    lynnej

moss-covered marker
three names
one date

    Gary Evans

at Seabeck
hearing the dinner bell
I long for Seabeck

    Michael Dylan Welch

weekend away
the sound of the sea
coming and going

    Susan Constable

light-scalloped water
all the mischief
we didn't get into

    Tanya McDonald

hearing the last low
call of crickets
sad thoughts of farewell

Ellen Ankenbrock

lights flicker—
the upper city drifts
on a fog ocean

Richard Tice

hills bring us home autumn dusk

Carmi Soifer

Kukai Winners

dim autumn sky

old age slipping into

all my hiding places

Michelle Schaefer

First Place

dim autumn sky
old age slipping into
all my hiding places

Michelle Schaefer

Second Place

the shadow of the jay
   deeper and deeper
      into the woods

Bob Redmond

Third Place

mismatched socks
his drawer overflowing
with memories

    David Berger

Fourth Place

allowing myself
to believe it might be different
distant peaks

    Bob Redmond

Fifth Place

fogbound morning
I arrive before
the geese

    C. R. Manley

Sixth Place

the whisper
of autumn leaves
his last goodbye

    Susan Constable

Seventh Place (tie)

alone . . .
even in the company
of a hundred crows

    Carole MacRury

the brush
loaded with ink
four centuries ago

    Jim Roberts

windy cemetery
a willow branch lays bare
a child's gravestone

    Seren Fargo

Seabeck Haiku Walk

mountain summit
how easily
reached
by
the
autumn
wind

Johnny Baranski

Ion Codrescu

mountain summit
how easily reached
by the autumn wind

    Johnny Baranski

a bit of something
falls from a tree
summer heat

    Seren Fargo

merry-go-round
yellow slickers whirling
in the rain

Marilyn Sandall

well-worn path—
I take my memories
for a walk

Carole MacRury

woodland path—
a small flower
bends our knees

    Connie Donleycott

rising toward
the slow turn of maple seeds
the child's laughter

    Richard Tice

on the bouncy bridge
an unknown force
rocks it

Ida Freilinger

the big dipper
no matter where I stand
mountain sky

Michelle Schaefer

warmed
by
the fire
not wanting
to be
older

or younger

Ion Codrescu   Francine Porad

Perseid shower—
tiny green apples
dot the lawn

    Carmen Sterba

warmed by the fire
not wanting to be older
or younger

    Francine Porad

rock throwing . . .
our circles
about to meet

    Alice Frampton

dinner bell—
the flip of a squirrel's tail
welcomes us

    Kathleen Tice

foghorns
we lower a kayak
into the sound

    Christopher Herold

meteor shower . . .
a gentle wave
wets our sandals

    Michael Dylan Welch

the metallic rasp
of a belted kingfisher . . .
morning mist

Angela Terry

morning snow—
tracks of animals
we never see

C. R. Manley

low tide . . .
the shells
not chosen

    Karma Tenzing Wangchuk

night sounds
from the lagoon
between snores

    Connie Hutchison

all our differences
forgotten—
full moon

    Tanya McDonald

silent Friends meeting
the sound of chairs being moved
to enlarge the circle

    Robert Major

Poets and Places

Kelly Sauvage Angel *Madison, Wisconsin*	27, 63
Ellen Ankenbrock *Washougal, Washington*	56, 67
Johnny Baranski (1948–2018) *Vancouver, Washington*	81
Theresa J. Barker *Seattle, Washington*	36, 50
David Berger *Seattle, Washington*	38, 63, 74
Susan M. Callan *Bainbridge Island, Washington*	27
Patricia Benedict Campbell *Houston, Texas*	54, 64
Terry Ann Carter *Victoria, British Columbia*	29, 51
Margaret Chula *Portland, Oregon*	30, 45
Rick Clark *Seattle, Washington*	40, 41
Ion Codrescu *Constanţa, Romania*	18, 26, 60
Susan Constable *Parksville, British Columbia*	56, 66, 75
Connie Donleycott *Bremerton, Washington*	83
Julie Emerson *Vancouver, British Columbia*	18, 54, 61
Gary Evans *Stanwood, Washington*	29, 65
Seren Fargo *Bellingham, Washington*	53, 60, 76, 81

Alice Frampton	88
Seabeck, Washington	
Marco Fraticelli	31, 60
Pointe Claire, Québec	
Mike Freiling	32, 49
Vancouver, Washington and *Kyoto, Japan*	
Ida Freilinger	38, 84
Redmond, Washington	
William Scott Galasso	28, 52
Laguna Woods, California	
Patrick Gallagher	27, 62
Anacortes, Washington	
Dianne Garcia	37, 51
Seattle, Washington	
Katharine Grubb	43, 50
Seattle, Washington	
Christopher Herold	89
Port Townsend, Washington	
Connie Hutchison	46, 59, 91
Kirkland, Washington	
Adam L. Kern	42, 45
Madison, Wisconsin	
Roy Kindelberger	35
Edmonds, Washington	
kjmunro (Katherine J. Munro)	19, 53, 55
Whitehorse, Yukon Territory	
lynnej (Lynne Jambor)	19, 30, 65
Vancouver, British Columbia	
Carole MacRury	53, 65, 76, 82
Point Roberts, Washington	
Robert Major (1920–2008)	92
Poulsbo, Washington	

C. R. Manley *Bellevue, Washington*	7, 28, 61, 75, 90
Vicki McCullough *Vancouver, British Columbia*	18, 31, 54
Tanya McDonald *Woodinville, Washington*	30, 66, 92
Jacquie Pearce *Vancouver, British Columbia*	19, 55, 62
Francine Porad (1929–2006) *Bellevue, Washington*	87
Joan Prefontaine *Cottonwood, Arizona*	41, 46
Laura Quindt *Woodinville, Washington*	31, 37
Bob Redmond *Burien, Washington*	26, 36, 73, 74
Jim Roberts *Victoria, British Columbia*	39, 76
jim rodriguez *Washougal, Washington*	32, 42
Jacob Salzer *Vancouver, Washington*	25, 59
Marilyn Sandall (1942–2015) *Seattle, Washington*	82
Paul Sarvasy *Bellingham, Washington*	40, 49
Michelle Schaefer *Bothell, Washington*	55, 63, 73, 84
Carole Slesnick *Bellingham, Washington*	50, 62
Crystal Simone Smith *Durham, North Carolina*	43, 56

Barbara Snow 26, 64
Eugene, Oregon

Carmi Soifer 39, 67
Suquamish, Washington

Sheila Sondik 28, 40
Bellingham, Washington

Marilyn Stablein 35, 61
Portland, Oregon

Carmen Sterba 38, 39, 87
University Place, Washington

John Stevenson 43, 45
Nassau, New York

R. J. Swanson 37, 44
Rollingbay, Washington

Angela Terry 44, 51, 90
Lake Forest Park, Washington

Kathleen I. Tice 32, 52, 88
Kent, Washington

Richard Tice 25, 67, 83
Kent, Washington

Diane Wallihan 41, 44
Port Townsend, Washington

Karma Tenzing Wangchuk 91
Port Townsend, Washington

Michael Dylan Welch 29, 66, 89
Sammamish, Washington

Garry Wilson 36, 52
Issaquah, Washington

Carolyn Winkler 42, 64
Portland, Oregon

www.ingramcontent.com/pod-product-compliance
Lightning Source LLC
Chambersburg PA
CBHW020948090426
42736CB00010B/1311